EXECUTIVE EDITORS
Sarah Galbraith, Alan Doan,
Jenny Doan, David Mifsud

MANAGING EDITOR

VIDEOGRAPHER
Jake Doan

TECHNICAL WRITER
Edie McGinnis

TECHNICAL EDITOR
Jane Miller

PATTERN LAYOUT
Ally Simmons

PROJECT DESIGN TEAM
Natalie Earnheart, Jenny Doan,
Sarah Galbraith

AUTHOR OF THE FAIR THIEF
Steve Westover

CONTRIBUTING COPY WRITERS
Jenny Doan, Natalie Earnheart, Christine
Ricks, Katie Mifsud, Cammille Maddox

COPY EDITOR
Nichole Spravzoff

CONTRIBUTING PIECERS
Jenny Doan, Natalie Earnheart,
Kelly McKenzie, Carol Henderson,
Cindy Morris

CONTRIBUTING QUILTERS
Jamey Stone-Quilting Department Manager,
Debbie Allen-Daytime Assistant Manager,
Tia Gilliam-Night Assistant Manager, Abby
Anderson, Betty Bates, Deloris Burnett,
Debbie Elder, James Evenson, Dixie Flamm,
Linda Frump, Bernice Kelly, Lori Parkey,
Sarah Richardson, Karen Russell, Kara Snow,
Tory Wood, Kayla Youtsey, Mari Zullig, Seth
Wynne, Devin Ragle, Janet Caselman

PRINTING SERVICES
Cenveo Publisher Services
2901 Byrdhill Road
Richmond, VA 23228

CONTACT US
Missouri Star Quilt Company
114 N Davis
Hamilton, Mo. 64644
888-571-1122
info@missouriquiltco.com

content

Ooops! Sometimes we make mistakes.
To find corrections to every issue of Block
go to: www.msqc.co/corrections

photo by Heidi Stock

hello
from MSQC

I love something about every season. I just choose to. I am not one of those people who wishes for winter the minute it gets warm, or for a sunny day while snow is falling down. I decide to love wherever I am and whatever I am doing—it's a good idea to bloom where you're planted! But there's something special about the onset of spring. I love it when I open the door one morning and, all of a sudden, I can feel spring coming.

One of my favorite things about spring is my Redbud tree. It's absolutely gorgeous. The flowers bloom first before the leaves and they are the most glorious color of pink you have ever seen! Spring is an ideal time to read outside on the back deck or enjoy a picnic on a quilt out in the grass. Warmer weather even makes me want to hang my clothes out on the line! As the garden begins to sprout, there's nothing better than filling the house with fresh flowers to bring the outside in. And of course, one of the best gifts of spring is the longer days, perfect for going on walks and riding bikes in the sunshine.

With so much to love about spring, let this amazing time of year fill your heart with new beginnings. Find time to enjoy the season and the beauty all around you. Let this time of year fill you up with inspiration on your quilting journey.

Jenny

JENNY DOAN
MISSOURI STAR QUILT CO

springing to *life*

Spring is here and I'm breathing in new life! New buds on the trees, new growth in the ground—all around me is bright and colorful! Spring in the air lifts my spirits and puts a spring in my step. I especially love the Magnolia tree. It's buds are so bold and striking against their dark branches. It makes me want to be the same in my creative life.

Taking cues from this glorious tree, I have pulled a bright, pastel color palette for our co-op this month, full of all the things that are stretching out their roots from winter's hibernation. Butterflies, buds, and a little gingham to set the mood for the possibility of a picnic in the near future. Whatever you're finding to work on these days, enjoy the rebirth of spring by letting it inspire your creativity too.

CHRISTINE RICKS
MSQC Creative Director, BLOCK MAGAZINE

SOLIDS

FBY12400 Kona Cotton - Daffodil
by Robert Kaufman Fabrics for Robert Kaufman
SKU: K001-148

FBY16237 Kona Cotton - Corsage
by Studio RK for Robert Kaufman by Studio RK
for Robert Kaufman
SKU: K001-487

FBY36111 Kona Cotton 2016 Color of the Year
by Robert Kaufman Fabrics for Robert Kaufman
SKU: K001-550

FBY12350 Kona Cotton - Azure
by Robert Kaufman Fabrics for Robert Kaufman
SKU: K001-1009

FBY16252 Kona Cotton - Pickle
by Studio RK for Robert Kaufman
SKU: K001-480

FBY3250 Kona Cotton - Natural
by Robert Kaufman Fabrics for Robert Kaufman
SKU: K001-1242

PRINTS

FBY29234 Carolina Gingham -
⅛" Woven Check Orange
by Robert Kaufman Fabrics for Robert Kaufman
SKU: P-5689-9

FBY36474 Dream Weaver - Beauty Mark Violet
by Amy Butler for Free Spirit Fabrics
SKU: PWAB157.VIOLE

FBY8499 Evening Blooms - Stripe Yellow
by Carina Gardner for Riley Blake
C3516-YELLOW

FBY13776 A Beautiful Thing - Butterfly Blue
by Zoe Pearn for Riley Blake
SKU: C3981-BLUE

FBY35986 Vintage Picnic - Smitten Green
by Bonnie & Camille for Moda Fabrics
SKU: 55127 14

FBY31843 Purebred - Preakness Sky
by Erin Michael for Moda Fabrics
SKU: 26092 20

disappearing
4-patch star

quilt designed by JENNY DOAN

The Disappearing 4-Patch Star was born out of a willingness to try something new. As with all of the "disappearing" blocks, I take a perfectly good finished block, chop it up, and rearrange it. At first it may seem wasteful or risky, but the results are always worth the gamble. Life is more rewarding, and a heck of a lot more fun, when you're willing to try something new!

Missouri Star Quilt Co. is a family business from start to finish—of course, as things got busier, that family has had to grow and expand to include a whole team of wonderful folks! Ron and I have seven talented children, and from Al's vast computer knowledge to Sarah's eye for design, we've put those talents to good use. Natalie works with BLOCK magazine and Hillary always has fun ideas to beautify our shops. But our son, Jake, has one of the most important behind-the-scenes jobs of all. Jake films and edits our YouTube tutorials. If you enjoy my videos, just know that Jake is right there with his camera every step of the way!

As you can imagine, Jake spends much of his time on the computer working on the videos, and his little ones seem to have caught the MSQC spirit! One day my four-year-old grandson,

For the tutorial and everything need you to make this quilt visit

www.msqc.co/blockspring16

8

Ezra, was in the studio watching Daddy work. Suddenly Ezra announced that he wanted to make a tutorial of his own. Grateful for a break from his work, Jake found a little stool for Ez to stand on and got everything ready on set, just the way it is when I am filming. Then it was lights, camera, action!

That sweet little Ezra took to the spotlight like a pro and began his introductions. Phrases like, "Take a look at this quilt behind me," came tumbling out of his little mouth as naturally as if he'd been hosting for years! As for the instructional portion of the tutorial, Ez went the simple route, "You just sew it, and hang it up!" Now that's my kind of quilt project!

After the video was released, I was flooded with viewer comments such as, "Watch out, Grandma! Someone's gunning for your job!" and "Uh oh, Jenny! Looks like there's a new quilting star in town!" For me, it was just so fun to see my little grandson imitate what he sees Grandma do every week.

Halting production to give a child the chance to play host may have seemed like a silly waste of time, but I sure am glad Jake was willing to take a break from his normal routine to give Ezra an opportunity to shine! Isn't that what life is all about? Go ahead, take a risk! Make your own path. Cut up those quilt blocks like a crazy person! I promise it'll all be worth it.

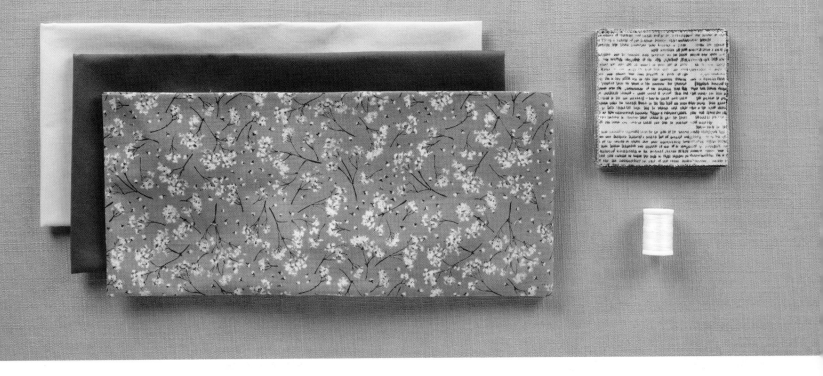

materials

makes an 82" X 94" quilt

QUILT TOP
- 2 packages 5″ print squares
- 1½ yards coordinating fabric
- 3½ yards background fabric – includes inner border

OUTER BORDER
- 1½ yards

BACKING
- 7½ yards

BINDING
- ¾ yard

SAMPLE QUILT
Wordsmith by Janet Clare for Moda

1 cut

From the coordinating yardage, cut:

- (5) 10″ strips across the width of the fabric – Subcut the strips into 10″ squares for a **total of 20 squares**.

From the background fabric, cut:

- (5) 10″ strips across the width of the fabric – Subcut the strips into 10″ squares for a **total of 20 squares.**

- (9) 4½″ strips across the width of the fabric – Subcut the strips into 4½″ squares for a **total of 80.**

- (3) 4½″ strips across the width of the fabric – Subcut the strips into 4½″ x 16½″ rectangles for a **total of 5 rectangles.**

2 make half-square triangles

Draw a line from corner to corner twice on the reverse side of each background 10″ square. Layer

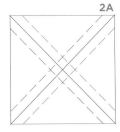

2A

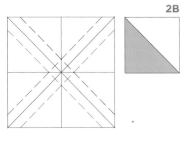

2B

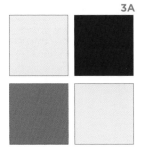

3A

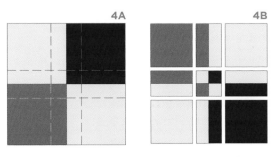

4A   4B

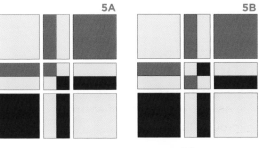

5A   5B

5C

a background square with a coordinating 10″ square with right sides facing. Sew ¼″ on either side of both drawn lines. **2A**

Cut through the center of the sewn squares horizontally and vertically. Then cut on the drawn lines. Each set of squares will yield 8 half-square triangle units. Trim to 4½″. You need a total of **160 units.** Set aside for the moment. **2B**

3 disappearing 4-patch center

Sew 2 contrasting 5″ print squares together. Repeat and sew the two together to make (1) 4-patch unit. **3A**

4 cut

If you have a rotating cutting mat, put the 4-patch block on it before making any cuts. If not, use a small cutting mat that can be easily picked up and turned.

Place the 1″ line of a rotary cutting ruler vertically on the center seam line. Cut along the edge of the ruler. **4A**

Turn the cutting mat without disturbing the pieces. Place the 1″ line of the ruler on the center seam line horizontally. Cut along the edge of the ruler. Continue on in this manner until you have made **4 cuts.** **4B**

5 trade

Swap the large squares at the top and bottom of the block that are directly across from each other. **5A**

Rotate the center 4-patch 90-degrees. **5B**

Sew the pieces back together into rows as shown. Sew the three rows together to complete the center of the block. **Make 20.** **5C**

6 block construction

Sew 2 half-square triangles together, making a flying geese unit. **Make 4.** **6A**

Sew a flying geese unit to either side of a center unit. **6B**

Stitch a 4½″ square to either side of a flying geese unit. Make 2 rows like this and sew one to the top and one to the bottom to complete the block. **Make 20.** **6C**

7 arrange in rows

Lay out your blocks in rows. Each row contains 4 blocks and you need 5 rows. After you are satisfied with the arrangement, sew the blocks together. Sew a 4½″ x 16½″ background strip to the beginning of rows 1, 3, and 5. Sew a 4½″ x 16½″ strip to the end of rows 2 and 4. Sew the rows together.

1 Layer a 10" background square with a contrasting 10" square. Draw a line from corner to corner twice on the diagonal. Sew ¼" on either side of the drawn lines. Cut the units apart by cutting through the center vertically and horizontally. Then cut on the drawn lines.

2 Sew (4) 5" contrasting squares together into a 4-patch.

3 Cut 1" from the center seam vertically, then horizontally. Continue on in this manner until you have made 4 cuts.

4 Trade the 4 corner pieces, then rotate the little center 4-patch 90-degrees.

5 Sew 2 half-square triangles together to make 1 flying geese unit. Make 4 per block.

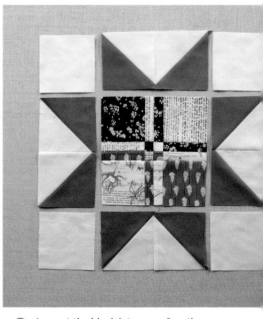

6 Lay out the block into rows. Sew the rows together to complete the block.

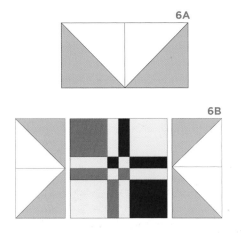

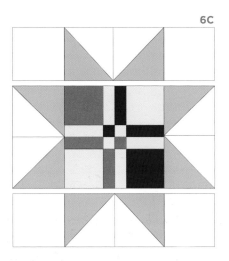

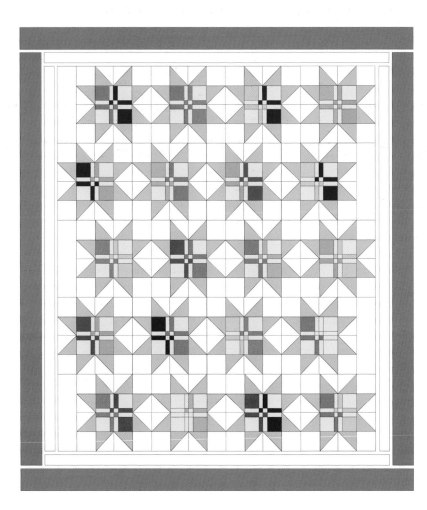

8 inner border

Cut (8) 2½" strips across the width of the fabric. Sew the strips together end-to-end to make one long strip. Trim the borders from this strip.

Refer to Borders (pg. 100) in the Construction Basics to measure and cut the outer borders. The strips are approximately 80½" for the sides and approximately 72½" for the top and bottom.

9 outer border

Cut (9) 5½" strips across the width of the fabric. Sew the strips together end-to-end to make one long strip. Trim the borders from this strip.

Refer to Borders (pg. 100) in the Construction Basics to measure and cut the outer borders. The strips are approximately 84½" for the sides and approximately 82½" for the top and bottom.

10 binding

Layer the quilt with backing and batting and quilt as desired. Square up and trim the excess batting and backing away. Add binding to finish. See Construction Basics (pg. 101) for binding instructions.

sashed half-hexagon

quilt designed by NATALIE EARNHEART

The Sashed Half-Hexagon quilt reminds me of a stained glass window. I absolutely adore how all those little framed pieces combine to create such a beautiful and interesting effect. But do you want to know the best part? It's all an illusion! Although this quilt appears to be complex and labor intensive, it's actually a piece of cake to put together! The secret is in the sashing.

Sashing is my weapon of choice when it comes to creating big impact for minimal effort. It's amazing how those simple little strips of fabric can change the look of a quilt. It's like framing a pretty picture. The sashing creates negative space and gives the block greater impact. Often I find it's the small things that really make all the difference.

When we moved our family from California to Missouri, we really had no idea what we were getting into. We sold our house and loaded all of our possessions into a moving truck, which Ron bravely drove across country. I followed behind him in the family van, full of excitable children, and Natalie, who was just sixteen years old at the time, took up the rear in her little, white car.

For the tutorial and everything you need to make this quilt visit:
www.msqc.co/blockspring16

Our journey across eight states took place in early March. For us Californians, March means springtime. What we didn't know was, throughout the Great Plains, March could be as meek as a lamb, or as ferocious as a lion. There might be snow on the ground, or blossoms on the trees.

It didn't take long before we encountered our first snowstorm. Oh, we had seen snow before, we had even driven through a flurry or two on our way to a sledding excursion, but we had never experienced the terror of traveling through a full-fledged blizzard. Endless snowflakes blurred my vision and the road was slick and difficult to navigate. I was a nervous wreck!

When we headed into Nebraska, the temperature actually got so low that the speedometer cable in the moving truck froze. Ron didn't know how

fast he was driving or how far he had traveled, but somehow we made it to Missouri in one piece and were able to start a new life for ourselves.

Life in California had been good, but as soon as I set foot on Missouri soil, I fell in love. It just felt like home! And each small victory, from learning to drive in the snow to figuring out how to light our old wood burning stove, enriched our lives and added color to our Missouri experience.

Little by little, those small moments change a person. Years have passed and I'm a true Missouri woman now—I can drive through the snow with the best of them! So whether you're adding a simple sashing to your quilt or braving an exciting new experience, remember, small things really do make all the difference!

 Here's another colorway of this block. Try different combinations of fabric to see which one you like best.

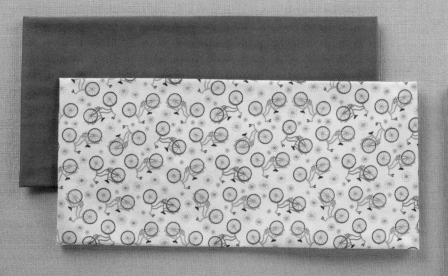

materials

makes a 50" X 63" quilt

QUILT TOP
- 1 package 10" squares
- 1½ yards sashing fabric – we used gray

BORDER
- 1 yard

BACKING
- 3¼ yards

BINDING
- ½ yard

ADDITIONAL SUPPLIES
- 1 MSQC 10" Half-Hexagon Template

SAMPLE QUILT
- **Sunday Ride** by Cheri Guidry for Benartex/Contempo

1 cut

Select (36) 10" squares from the package.

- Cut each in half, making 5" x 10" rectangles for a **total of 72.**

From the sashing fabric, cut:

- (72) 1½" x 12" strips

2 trim

Place the Half-Hexagon Template on top of each of the 5" x 10" rectangles. Trim around the template. **2A**

TEMPLATE

2A

2B

2C

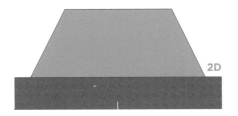

2D

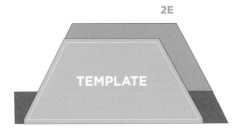

2E

TEMPLATE

2F

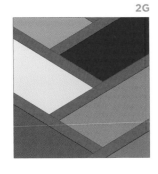

2G

Fold a half-hexagon piece in half and press a crease (just use your fingers) at the halfway point on the widest edge. 2B

Fold a 1½" sashing strip in half and finger press a crease in the half-hexagon piece and the sashing strip. 2C

Match up the halfway point creases in the half-hexagon piece and the sashing strip with right sides facing. Pin and sew the two pieces together. The sashing strip will extend past the edges of the hexagon piece. 2D

After you have sewn the two pieces together, press the sashing away from the half-hexagon. Place the half-hexagon template back on the piece. Align the side edge of the template with the side of the print hexagon and the bottom of the gray sashing strip and trim the gray strip. Repeat for the other side of the half-hexagon. **Make 6** for each block, a **total of 72.** 2E

Sew the sashed half-hexagons together by following diagram 2F. **Make 12.**

Trim the blocks to 12½" square. 2G

3 lay out and sash

From the sashing fabric, cut:

- (8) 1½" x 12½" strips

- 5) 1½" x 38½" strips

- (3) 1½" x WOF – sew these strips together to make one long strip. You will cut the strips for the two sides from this strip (approximately 53½" for each side).

Lay out the blocks in **4 rows of 3.** Once you are happy with the arrangement, begin sewing the blocks together, adding a vertical sashing strip between each block. 3A

After the blocks are sewn together into rows, sew the rows together. Measure the rows across (approximately 38½") and add a 1½" long strip between each row. Sew a long strip to the top and the bottom of the blocks as well. Refer to the quilt diagram on page 23 if necessary.

Measure the quilt through the center vertically (approximately 53½") and sew a 1½" strip that length to either side of the quilt.

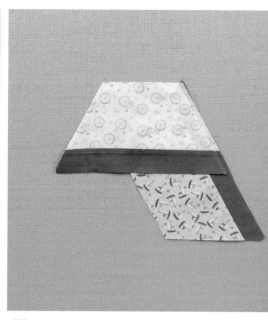

1 Fold a 10″ square in half. Align the large half-hexagon template with the raw edge and cut around the template to make 2 half-hexagons.

2 Sew a 1½″ strip to the long edge of the half-hexagon.

3 Begin sewing the pieces together. Start with the shortest seam as shown.

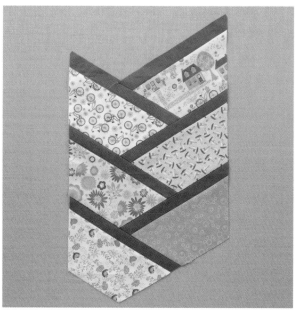

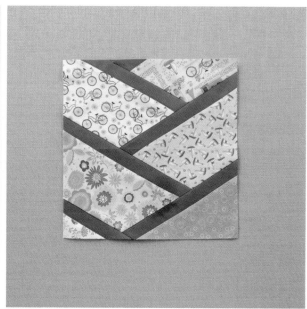

4 Sew 6 half-hexagons together.

5 Trim the block to 12½″.

4 border

Cut (6) 5½" strips across the width of the fabric. Sew the strips together end-to-end to make one long strip. Trim the borders from this strip. Refer to Borders (pg. 100) in the Construction Basics to measure and cut the outer borders. The strips are approximately 53½" for the sides and approximately 50½" for the top and bottom.

5 quilt and bind

Layer the quilt with batting and backing and quilt. After the quilting is complete, square up the quilt and trim away all excess batting and backing. Add binding to complete the quilt. See Construction Basics (pg. 101) for binding instructions.

*For the tutorial and everything
you need to make this quilt visit:*
www.msqc.co/blockspring16

ingrid's garden

quilt designed by NATALIE EARNHEART

One of my favorite old quilt patterns is Grandmother's Flower Garden. I am a sucker for antiques, and I have several Grandmother's Flower Garden quilts in my collection that I've acquired over the years. I love to study the intricate hexagons pieced together to form each flower and just imagine the hours of careful work that went into putting together such breathtaking designs. It's inspiring to see the different color choices, and how, oftentimes, the middle of the flower has been fussy cut to position a special print perfectly in the center. I have always loved to garden and fill my yard with beautiful plants, and there's something magical about these quilted flowers that inspire generation after generation.

My grandmother Ingrid wasn't a quilter, but she was passionate about flowers. Over the years, she sketched and embroidered countless flowers, but the most beautiful blooms of all were those she grew in her own garden. For most of her life, Grandma maintained a large and beautiful garden that was the envy of the whole neighborhood. As she got older, it became necessary for her to move in with my family, so she had to leave her garden behind, and she learned the art of indoor gardening.

In no time at all, Grandma had filled our home with beautiful, thriving plants. If there was a shelf, a window sill, or a tabletop, you can bet Grandma had made it the home of a potted flower or two. Grandma was especially drawn to unusual and unique looking plants, and every new bud or leaf was a source of great excitement. I loved all of her plants, but I was always most drawn to her vast collection of African violets. Those violets were amazing! She had variations that bloomed in just about every color of

the rainbow. It may seem a little silly, but Grandma and I could talk for hours about her beloved plants. I supposed it takes a certain kind of person to love a plant so much that it becomes a topic of engaging conversation! I've always said that I inherited my green thumb from her, and I treasure those moments I spent with Grandma and her plants.

When we decided to make a Grandmother's Flower Garden quilt, it seemed natural to name it after my grandma, Ingrid. Every time I see these beautiful, everlasting petals, I am reminded of her and everything she taught me about gardening. How I miss her!

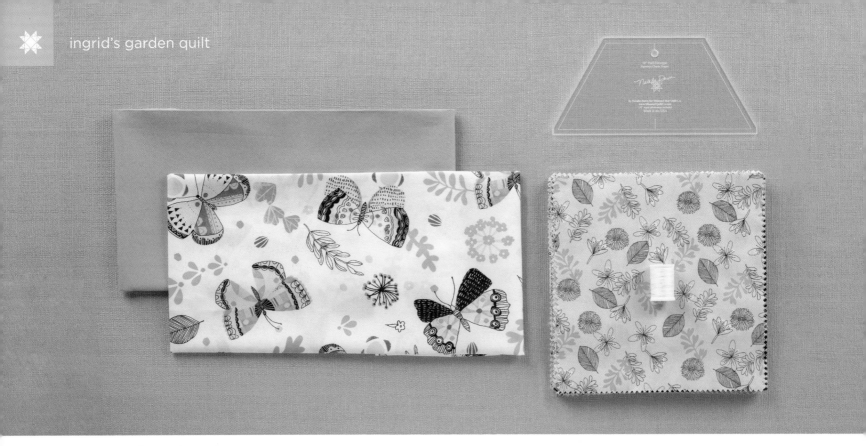

materials

makes a 92" X 106¼" quilt

QUILT TOP
- 2 packages 10" print squares
- 4 yards solid – includes inner border

OUTER BORDER
- 2 yards

BACKING
- 8¼ yards

BINDING
- ¾ yard

ADDITIONAL SUPPLIES
- 1 MSQC 10" Half-Hexagon Template

SAMPLE QUILT
- **Whisper** by Victoria Johnson for Windham

1 cut

From print squares, cut:
- 156 half-hexagons – Fold (78) 10" squares in half. Place the long edge of the Half-Hexagon template along the raw edges of each square. Cut around the shape to make 2 half-hexagons. **1A**

From solid, cut:
- (11) 10" strips across the width of the fabric. Fold each of the strips in half lengthwise and cut **86 half-hexagons. 1B**

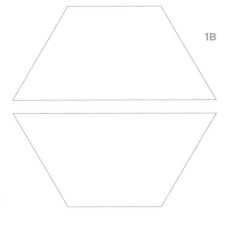

↓ FOLD ↓   1A

1B

2A

3 inner border

Cut (9) 2½" strips across the width of the fabric. Sew the strips together end-to-end to make one long strip. Trim the borders from this strip.

Refer to Borders (pg. 100) in the Construction Basics to measure and cut the inner borders. The strips are approximately 91¼" for the sides and approximately 80½" for the top and bottom.

4 outer border

Cut (10) 6½" strips across the width of the fabric. Sew the strips together end-to-end to make one long strip. Trim the borders from this strip.

Refer to Borders (pg. 100) in the Construction Basics to measure and cut the outer borders. The strips are approximately 95¼" for the sides and approximately 92½" for the top and bottom.

2 layout and sew

Lay out the half-hexagons as show in the assembly diagram. 2A

Make **22 rows** and sew the rows together.

After all the rows are sewn together, trim the side edges so they are straight.

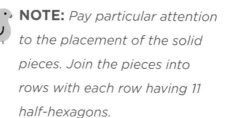 **NOTE:** *Pay particular attention to the placement of the solid pieces. Join the pieces into rows with each row having 11 half-hexagons.*

5 binding

Layer the quilt with batting and backing and quilt. After the quilting is complete, square up the quilt and trim away all excess batting and backing. Add binding to complete the quilt. See Construction Basics (pg. 101) for binding instructions.

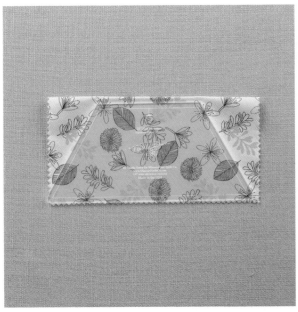

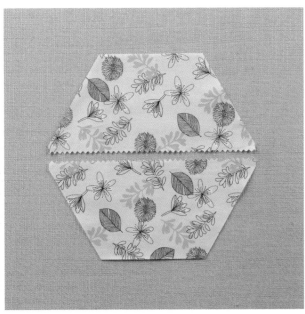

2 Fold a 10″ square in half. Align the long edge of the half-hexagon template along the raw edges of the folded square and cut around the template.

3 Each 10″ square will yield 2 half-hexagons.

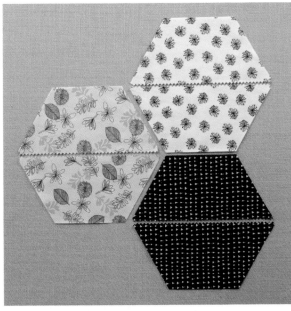

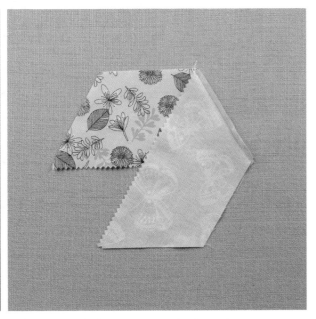

5 Sew the half-hexagons together into rows. Be aware of color placement so each half-hexagon forms a complete hexagon when the row is sewn together.

6 Join one half-hexagon to another by sewing on the diagonal. When the piece is opened and pressed, it will lie flat and form a straight row.

For the tutorial and everything
you need to make this quilt visit:
www.msqc.co/blockspring16

4-patch
& strips

quilt designed by JENNY DOAN

Moving to Missouri was a big adjustment for my kids. I don't know if the phrase "culture shock" quite conveys the feeling. They went from having a lot of friends and loads of things to do to suddenly having only a handful of kids around to play with and living a quiet life on a farm in the middle of nowhere.

It didn't bother me, as I can make my own fun, but that's a learned skill, of course, and the kids just hadn't learned it yet. They always seemed to be looking for reasons to drive to town where there was more going on, or so they thought. One common request was, "Let's go to the movies!" But the closest movie theater was an hour away, and that's a big deal when you drive a full-size, gas-guzzling van that gets ten miles to the gallon.

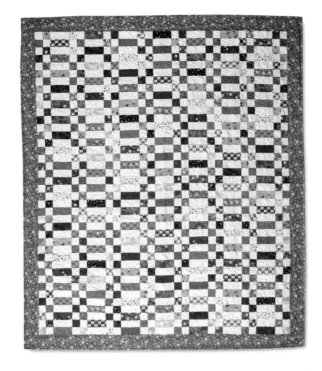

One night the kids were asking about going to the movies again and we just didn't have the money. You know, I'm always looking for ways to say yes, so I suggested a drive-in movie. The kids were confused, protesting, "But they don't have those here." "No problem," I said, "Who needs a real drive-in when you've got a nice, big lawn?"

I sent the kids off to invite their friends over and we spread quilts all over the grass. All we had to do was haul out the TV and VCR to the front porch and voila! Our yard became an open-air theater! We popped buckets and buckets of popcorn and lay out under the stars. Popcorn, friends, cozy quilts, and a simple movie turned into the best night at the drive-in we'd ever had.

"Popcorn, friends, cozy quilts, and a simple movie turned into the best night at the drive-in we'd ever had."

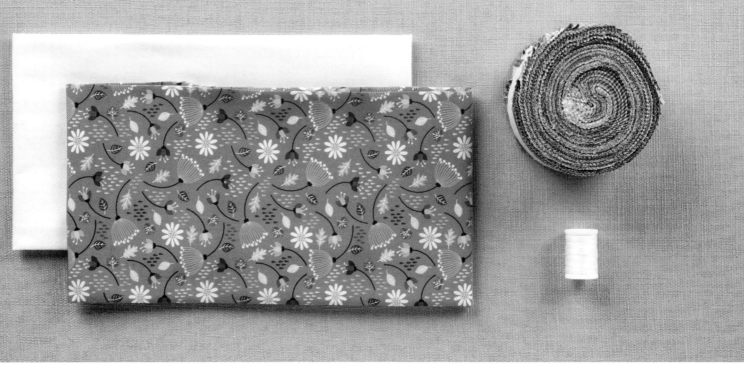

materials

makes a 75" x 88" quilt

QUILT TOP
- 1 roll print 2½" strips
- 1 roll background 2½" strips *or*
  3 yards background fabric

BORDER
- 1¼ yards

BACKING
- 5½ yards

BINDING
- ¾ yard

SAMPLE QUILT
- **Enchanted** by Alisse Courter
  for Camelot

1 sew
Sew a background 2½" strip to a print 2½" strip to make a strip set. **Make 40. 1A**

2 cut
From 20 strip sets, cut:

- (7) 5½" wide increments for a **total of 140. 2A**

From 20 strip sets, cut:

- (16) 2½" wide increments for a **total of 320. 2B**

Sew (2) 2½" strip set increments together to make (1) 4-patch unit. **Make 160. 2C**

Block Size: 4-Patch: 4" finished

Strips: 4" x 5" finished

1A

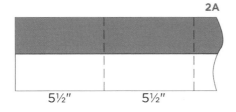

2A

5½"   5½"

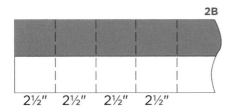

2B

2½"   2½"   2½"   2½"

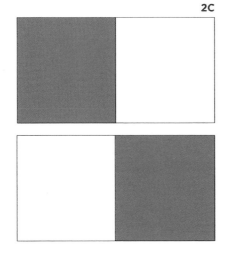

2C

3 lay out and sew

Lay out the 4-patches and the strips in rows, alternating the two blocks. You will have (8) 4-patches alternating with 7 strip blocks in each row horizontally. Notice the print portion of the 4-patch always touches a background portion of a strip block. **Make 20 rows. 3A**

Sew the rows together to complete the center of the quilt.

4 borders

Cut (8) 4½" strips across the width of the fabric. Sew the strips together end-to-end to make one long strip. Trim the borders from this strip.

Refer to Borders (pg. 100) in the Construction Basics to measure and cut the outer borders. The strips are approximately 80½" for the sides and approximately 75½" for the top and bottom.

5 binding

Layer the quilt with backing and batting and quilt as desired. Square up and trim the excess batting and backing away. Add binding to finish. See the Construction Basics (pg. 101) for binding instructions.

3A

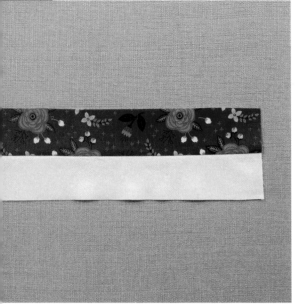

1 Sew a background strip to a print strip.

2 Cut 20 strips into 2½" increments.

3 Cut 20 strips into 5½" increments.

4 Sew (2) 2-patch units together to make a 4-patch.

5 Lay out a 4-patch unit and a strip unit. Be sure the print on the 4-patch will be sewn to the background portion of the strip unit.

6 Sew the 4-patch unit to the strip to complete one block.

For the tutorial and everything you need to make this quilt visit: **www.msqc.co/blockspring16**

tangled
geese

quilt designed by JENNY DOAN

If you've never been canoeing, it's time to get out on the water, darlin', and get paddling! Some of our best family adventures happened on the river, and I wouldn't trade one of them, even the ones where I ended up soaking wet!

Every canoe trip was a special event for us, and it ran like clockwork, most of the time. We packed up the kids and all our gear into the trusty van and headed out to the Niangua River—heaven only knows how we fit nine of us and all our stuff inside! Once we got there, I always loved setting up camp; we made the space our own by arranging our three tents in a circle around the fire, facing each other. There was one tent for the girls, one for the boys, and one for Ron and me. In contrast to cooking at home, fixing dinner around a campfire hardly felt like work, it was just so relaxing being outdoors. After a pleasant evening around the fire, roasting marshmallows and singing camp songs, everybody would head to bed, excited for the next day's adventure.

As you are probably aware, teenagers can't be roused from sleep easily; they'd probably sleep through a volcano explosion! But on a canoe trip, the kids were always up early, full of energy and anxious to get on the river. You couldn't ask for a better river for kids to learn on than the Niangua. With gentle rapids and plenty of opportunities to paddle, we felt safe, but it kept us busy. Of course the kids found time to argue anyway, and whenever that happened I would yell "Switch!" The kids knew the drill: at least one person had to get out of their boat and get into another one. It's a good thing all the children knew how to swim! The system worked pretty well for discipline until it got too hot and everybody wanted to cool off in the river anyway.

We made a lot of great memories out there on the river, and learned a few important lessons. I remember one day I was in a canoe with Alan and he yelled, "Mom! Duck!" I dove down just in time to miss a tree branch brushing over me. Catching a branch in the face wouldn't have been very pleasant! I also remember when I was canoeing with Josh and we hit a rock. The poor boy was catapulted into the air! Somehow he grabbed a passing tree branch and hung on for dear life, which left me alone in the canoe. You can imagine what happened next. With his weight suddenly gone, the end flipped straight up—before I knew it I was in the river!

We all survived and I'll never forget the laughs we had playing canoe tag and racing each other down the river. There was even a rope swing where we could pull off and stop for a bit of fun. We were always disappointed when we reached the spot where the bus came to pick us up and we had to get out of the river, putting an end to that day's adventures. I'll always treasure those happy memories, paddling along in a canoe.

materials

makes a 70" X 78" quilt

QUILT TOP
- 1 roll print 2½" strips
- 4¼ yards background fabric – includes inner border

OUTER BORDER
- 1½ yards

BACKING
- 4¾ yards

BINDING
- ¾ yard

SAMPLE QUILT
- **Circle Play** by Ann Lauer for Benartex

1 cut

From each of the print strips, cut:

- (6) 2½" x 4½" rectangles
- (6) 2½" squares

From the background fabric, cut:

- (53) 2½" strips across the width of the fabric - subcut 25 strips into 4½" rectangles for a **total of 224**. Cut the remaining strips into 2½" squares for a **total of 448.**

2 block construction

Select (2) 2½" x 4½" rectangles and (2) 2½" squares of a print

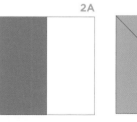
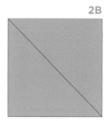
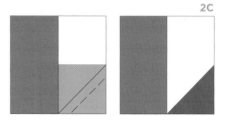

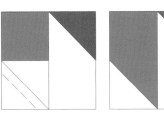

2D

2E

2F

2G

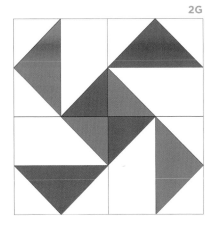

(Print #1). Select the same from print #2. Set aside the 2½" squares of print #1 and the 4½" rectangles of print #2.

Sew a 2½" x 4½" print #1 rectangle to a 2½" x 4½" background rectangle. **Make 2 units** per block. 2A

Draw a line from corner to corner on the reverse side of (2) 2½" print #2 squares and (4) 2½" background squares. 2B

Place a 2½" print #2 square on the lower right corner of the unit and sew on the drawn line. Trim the excess fabric ¼" away from the sewn seam. Open and press. 2C

Place a 2½" background square on the upper left corner of the unit and sew on the drawn line. Trim the excess fabric ¼" away from the sewn seam. Open and press. 2D

Place a 2½" background square on the lower left corner of the unit and sew on the drawn line. Trim the excess fabric ¼" away from the sewn seam. Open and press the two identical units. 2E

Repeat using the print #2 rectangles and print #1 squares that were set aside and make the two remaining units for the block. 2F

Sew the 4 units together as shown to complete the block. 2G

Make 56 blocks.

Block Size: 8" finished

3 lay out

Set the blocks together into rows with each row having **7 blocks** across. **Make 8 rows.** Press the seam allowances of the even numbered rows toward the left and the odd numbered rows toward the right. This will make the seams nest.

4 inner border

Cut (7) 2½" strips across the width of the fabric. Sew the strips together end-to-end to make one long strip. Trim the borders from this strip.

Refer to Borders (pg. 100) in the Construction Basics to measure and cut the inner borders. The strips are approximately 64½" for the sides and approximately 60½" for the top and bottom.

5 outer border

Cut (8) 5½" strips across the width of the fabric. Sew the strips together end-to-end to make one

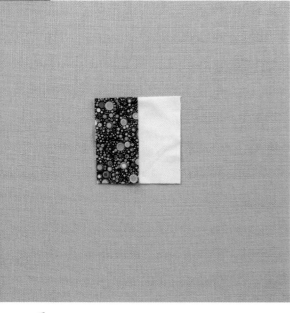

1 Sew a background rectangle to a print rectangle.

2 Place a 2½" print square on the lower right corner of the unit and sew on the drawn line. Trim the excess fabric ¼" away from the sewn seam.

3 Place a background 2½" square on the upper left corner of the unit and sew on the drawn line. Trim the excess fabric away ¼" from the sewn line.

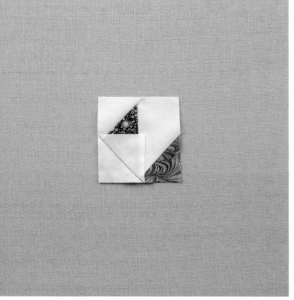

4 Sew a background 2½" square to the lower left corner of the unit. Sew on the drawn line and trim ¼" away from the sewn line. This completes one quadrant of the block.

5 Make 4 quadrants using print #1 and print #2. Each unit is made the same, only the color placement changes.

6 Sew the 4 quadrants together to complete the block.

long strip. Trim the borders from this strip.

Refer to Borders (pg. 100) in the Construction Basics to measure and cut the outer borders. The strips are approximately 68½″ for the sides and approximately 70½″ for the top and bottom.

6 quilt and bind

Layer the quilt with batting and backing and quilt. After the quilting is complete, square up the quilt and trim away all excess batting and backing. Add binding to complete the quilt. See Construction Basics (pg. 101) for binding instructions.

For the tutorial and everything you need to make this quilt visit:

www.msqc.co/blockspring16

quatrefoil
star

quilt designed by JENNY DOAN

This is a twist on the traditional Quatrefoil quilt pattern. With one turn, a whole new block appears! It's just another example of the importance of one little thing. Small changes can make all the difference. Just ask my daughter, Sarah, about the power of a great pair of shoes, in just the right color, and she'll agree!

When our daughter, Sarah, was a little girl she adored anything purple, though she couldn't quite say her R's yet and called it "puhple," which made it even cuter. With Sarah it had to be the "puhple" cup at lunch and the "puhple" marker for coloring and the "puhple" shirt every day of the week, whether or not it had spaghetti on it from last night's dinner, thank you very much.

Sarah's love of purple reached its crowning moment when Aunt Ingie came to town for a visit. I love my Aunt Ingie, she is an awesome person. She used to travel the world, working with

archaeologists in the most incredible places. She often sent me postcards from exotic lands and I wanted to be just like her.

Every once in a while, Aunt Ingie would come out for a visit, and she was great fun to have around. The kids always got so excited to see her—in part because she always brought a bag full of coins to share with them. She let the children reach into the bag and grab as much money as they could hold in their little fists. It was totally magical to them.

Sarah and Aunt Ingie were like two peas in a pod, they just had a great time together. And on one of Ingie's visits, she decided to take Sarah shopping. Sarah was about five at the time, but that doesn't stop a doting aunt from taking her niece out on the town! So when they came home, Sarah had on a purple pair of high heels with a purse to match, and a huge grin on her face. I'd never seen a child so in love with a pair of shoes! Sarah was in purple heaven! All through playtime, bath time, and bedtime, Sarah couldn't bear to be parted from her big girl, "puhple" heels. Those little pumps transformed her whole world. It took an awful lot of convincing to keep Sarah from climbing in the tub, purple heels and all—and she may have slept with them on that night. Even though she outgrew them long ago, and she stopped saying "puhple," I bet Sarah would love to see her beloved purple heels again.

" This is a twist on the traditional Quatrefoil quilt pattern. With one turn, a whole new block appears! It's just another example of the power of one little thing. "

materials
makes a 74" X 86" quilt

QUILT TOP
- 4 packages of 5″ print squares
- 2¾ yards white – includes inner border
- 1¼ yards coordinating print

OUTER BORDER
- 1¼ yards

BACKING
- 5¼ yards

BINDING
- ¾ yard

SAMPLE QUILT
- **Bees 'n Blooms** by Kansas Troubles for Moda

1 cut
From the white fabric, cut:

- (30) 2½″ strips across the width of the fabric – subcut 15 of the strips into 2½″ squares for a **total of 240**. Set aside the remaining **15 strips** for the moment.

From the coordinating print fabric, cut:

- (15) 2½″ strips across the width of the fabric.

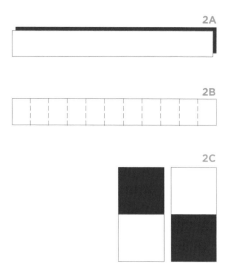

3A

3B

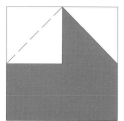

2 make 4-patch units

Make a strip set by sewing a 2½" print strip to a 2½" white strip. Press the seam allowance toward the darkest fabric. Repeat for the remaining 2½" strips for a **total of 15 strip sets.** 2A

Cut each strip set into 2½" increments. You should have (16) 2-patch units per strip set. 2B

Sew (2) 2-patch units together to make (1) 4-patch unit. **Make (120) 4-patch units.** 2C

3 make star point units

Select 4 matching 5" print squares. Trim each to 4½".

Fold (8) 2½" squares once on the diagonal and press. The crease will mark your sewing line. 3A

Position a 2½" square on one corner of a 4½" square. Sew along the crease, trim the excess fabric away ¼" from the sewn seam and press. Repeat for the adjacent side of the square. **Make 4 star point units per block.** Keep each matching set of star points together. You'll need **30 sets of 4** for the quilt. 3B

4 block construction

Each block consists of 3 rows.

Trim (30) 5" squares to 4½" to use in the center of the blocks.

4A

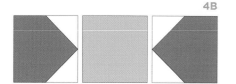

4B

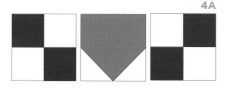

Sew a 4-patch unit to either side of a star point unit. Make 2 rows like this. 4A

Sew a star point unit to either side of a 4½" center square. Make 1 row like this. 4B

Sew the 3 rows together to complete the block. **Make 30 blocks.** 4C

Block Size: 12" Finished

4C

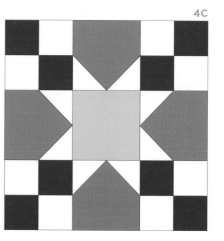

5 arrange in rows

Lay out the blocks in rows, with each row made up of **5 blocks.** You need **6 rows.** When you are happy with the appearance, sew the blocks together. Press the odd numbered rows toward the right and the even numbered rows toward the left to make the seams nest. Sew the rows together.

6 inner border

Cut (7) 2½" strips across the width of the fabric. Sew the strips together end-to-end to make one long strip. Trim the borders from this strip.

1 Sew (2) 2½″ strips together. Subcut the strips into 2½″ increments.

2 Sew (2) 2-patches together to make a 4-patch.

3 Place a marked 2½″ background square on one corner of a 4½″ square. Sew on the line and trim ¼″ away from the sewn seam.

4 Sew another marked 2½″ background square onto the 4½″ square and trim ¼″ away from the sewn line.

5 Make (4) star points for each block.

6 Sew the 4-patches and star points together to complete the block.

Refer to Borders (pg. 100) in the Construction Basics to measure and cut the inner borders. The strips are approximately 72½" for the sides and approximately 64½" for the top and bottom.

7 outer border

Cut (8) 5½" strips across the width of the fabric. Sew the strips together end-to-end to make one long strip. Trim the borders from this strip.

Refer to Borders (pg. 100) in the Construction Basics to measure and cut the outer borders. The strips are approximately 76½" for the sides and approximately 74½" for the top and bottom.

8 quilt and bind

Layer the quilt with backing and batting and quilt as desired. Square up and trim the excess batting and backing away. Add binding to finish. See Construction Basics (pg. 101) for binding instructions.

ohio *star*

quilt designed by JENNY DOAN

The Ohio Star quilt pattern dates back to the early 1800s. You may know it by a few different names including "Variable Star," "Lone Star," "Western Star," and others. It's a classic block and it seems that each new generation of quilters has discovered this beautiful pattern and fallen in love with it all over again. Of course, like so many traditional blocks, the Ohio Star might seem a bit complicated at first, but this pattern will help you feel confident to give it a try!

I have always loved antique quilts, and when I look at those detailed patterns, I feel so inspired imagining how much work went into putting them together. I can picture the quilter meticulously cutting each piece by hand and building blocks stitch by stitch with a needle and thread. My hands start to ache just thinking about it! As you know, I'm always looking ways to simplify the quilting process, so I have a lot of respect for traditional quilters!

For the tutorial and everything you need to make this quilt visit:
www.msqc.co/blockspring16

56

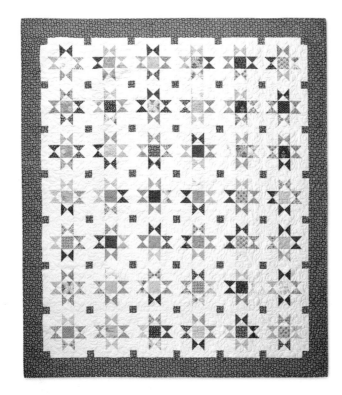

When I first found an interest in quilting, I turned to my 89-year-old neighbor, Mildred, for help. She was delighted at the opportunity to share her skill and wisdom with me. When I wondered how much fabric I would need, Mildred assured me that real quilting is done exclusively with scraps. "Should I bring my sewing machine over?" I asked. "Oh no, honey," she replied, "We won't use a sewing machine. I quilt by hand."

Quilt by hand? That phrase practically scared me off right then! Although I treasure my time spent with Mildred, she was never able to convince me to leave my sewing machine behind. Sometimes I do regret missing out on the experience of traditional quilting, but then I remember how much I love quick and simple solutions. I'm a sucker for modern conveniences, especially those that help me quilt!

I'm always on a quest to find easier ways to build those often perplexing, yet beautiful, traditional quilt blocks. I had been working on the Ohio Star pattern for quite a while, hoping to make it work with precuts, and I'm thrilled with this simplified pattern! I've heard it said that quilting quickly betrays the integrity of the art, but in this fast-paced world, I'm grateful to help even the busiest of folks enjoy such a fulfilling, creative hobby. It is truly wonderful to be able to sit down at the sewing machine for an afternoon and come away with something beautiful and handmade.

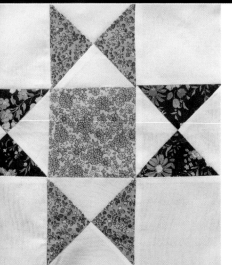

 Here's another colorway of this block. Try different combinations of fabric to see which one you like best.

materials

makes an 88" x 100½" quilt

QUILT TOP
- 3 packages (42 count) 5" print squares
- 6 yards background fabric – includes sashing strips

BORDER
- 2 yards - includes cornerstones

BACKING
- 8 yards

BINDING
- ¾ yard

SAMPLE QUILT
- **Beaujolais** by Sue Daley Designs

1 cut

Trim (42) 5" print squares to 4".

From the background fabric, cut:

- (11) 5" strips across the width of the fabric – Subcut the strips into 5" squares for a **total of 84.**

- (17) 4" strips across the width of the fabric – Subcut the strips into 4" squares for a **total of 168.**

2 make block units

Draw a line from corner to corner once on the diagonal on the reverse side of a 5" background square. **2A**

Layer the background square with a 5" print square with right sides facing. Sew ¼" on both sides of the drawn line. **2B**

Cut the square in half by cutting on the drawn line. **2C**

Open and press the seam toward the darker color. Each yields 2 half-square triangles. **2D**

Draw a line from corner to corner once on the diagonal on one of the half-square triangles. **2E**

Place the half-square triangle atop a matching half-square triangle with right sides and opposite colors facing. The seams will nest.

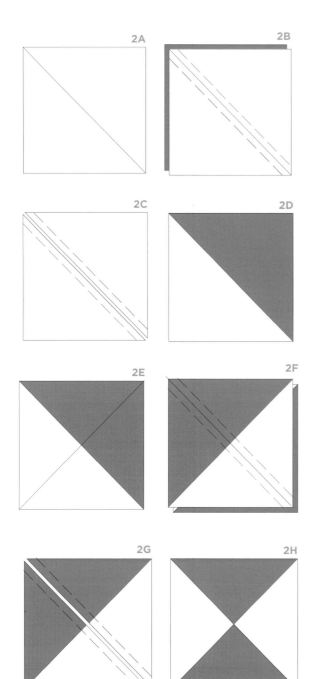

Sew ¼" on either side of the drawn line. **2F**

Cut the square in half by cutting on the diagonal drawn line. **2G**

Open and press the seam toward the darkest color. Each yields 2 hourglass blocks. **Make 168 units** and trim each to 4". **2H**

3 block construction

Sew a 4" background square to either side of an hourglass unit. Make 2 rows like this. **3A**

Sew an hourglass unit to either side of a 4" print square. Make one row like this. **3B**

Sew the 3 rows together to complete the block. **Make 42 blocks.** **3C**

Block Size: 10½" finished

4 cut sashing strips

From the background sashing fabric, cut:

- (33) 2½" strips across the width of the fabric. Subcut each of the strips into (3) 2½" x 11" rectangles. You'll need a **total of 97.**

5 cut cornerstones

From the border fabric, cut:

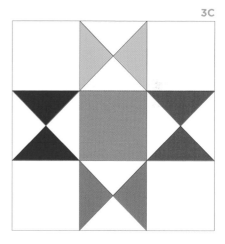

- (4) 2½" strips across the width of the fabric. Subcut the strips into (56) 2½" squares.

6 arrange and sew

Lay out the blocks in rows, with each row containing **6 blocks.** Place a 2½" x 11" background sashing rectangle at the beginning and end of each row as well as a rectangle between each block. **Make 7 rows.** Press all seams toward the blocks. **6A**

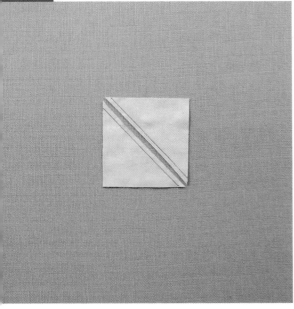

1 Draw a line from corner to corner on the diagonal on the reverse side of a background 5" square. Layer the background square with a print 5" square and sew on either side of the drawn line. Cut on the drawn line.

2 Press the half-square triangles open.

3 Draw a line from corner to corner once on the diagonal of one of the half-square triangles. Place it atop a matching half-square triangle with right sides and opposite colors facing. Sew on either side of the drawn line. Cut apart on the line.

4 Open each unit and press. Trim each hourglass unit to 4".

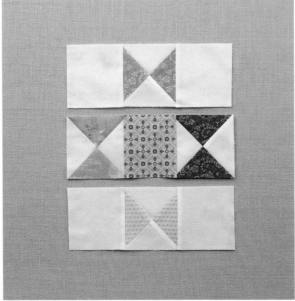

5 Sew the units into rows.

6 Sew the three rows together to complete the block.

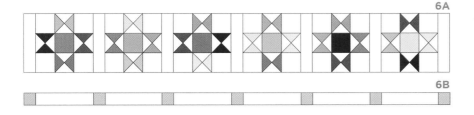

7 sashing strips

Sew a 2½" square (cornerstone) to a 2½" x 11" background rectangle. Add a 2½" square, then another background rectangle. Continue on in this manner until you have sewn a strip containing 7 cornerstones and 6 rectangles. **Make 8 sashing strips.** Press all seams toward the cornerstones. 6B

Sew a sashing strip between each row of blocks. Finish the center of the quilt by sewing one sashing strip to the top of the quilt and one to the bottom.

8 outer border

Cut (9) 6" strips across the width of the fabric. Sew the strips together end-to-end to make one long strip.

Refer to Borders (pg. 100) in the Construction Basics to measure and cut the borders. The strips for the sides are approximately 90" and the strips for the top and bottom are approximately 88½".

9 quilt and bind

Layer the quilt with backing and batting and quilt as desired. Square up and trim the excess batting and backing away. Add binding to finish. See Construction Basics (pg. 101) for binding instructions.

For the tutorial and everything you need to make this quilt visit:

www.msqc.co/blockspring16

friendship
pinwheel

quilt designed by JENNY DOAN

When my granddaughter Allyson turned sixteen, the only thing she wanted for her birthday was a princess themed party. Yes, you read that right. My sixteen-year-old darling is still a princess through and through, and as luck would have it, so are her friends. All nine of these teenage girls decided to dress up as Disney princesses and spend an entire day basking in royal elegance. And that's not all! They also decided to make it a community event and invite young children from the neighborhood to come and celebrate along with them. The little ones were delighted to spend time with "real" princesses!

Allyson's mother, Hillary, has been sewing for years, but even for an experienced seamstress it was quite the undertaking to construct nine princess gowns with big, fluffy skirts and all manner of bows, jewels, and royal accessories. The weeks leading up to the big event were filled with endless stitching, fittings, alterations, and more fittings. Hillary's sewing room began to look like a rainbow exploded everywhere in a shower of colorful glitter and frills.

On the day of the party, last minute adjustments were still being made as the girls started to arrive. Happy chaos ensued as they got to work transforming themselves amid piles of high heels, costume jewelry, and shimmering tiaras.

With the last earring in place, the girls were finally ready. They looked truly beautiful, just like real-life princesses! And you could tell that they felt different. There was something in the way they walked that gave them an air of refinement and dignity, with a giggle here and there for good measure. The girls piled into the minivan, puffy skirts billowing up to their tiaras, and rode over to the local park where they were delighted to discover that several of their male friends had decided to dress up as princes and join in on the fun!

Pretty soon little boys and girls from all over town started to show up to meet their favorite princesses. Allyson and her friends had a ball interacting with those little ones, and it wasn't long before they forgot all about their own party and became completely consumed with the magic of making memories that would last a lifetime for those children.

Good friends are hard to find, especially for teenagers. For better or for worse, friends have such an impact on the lives of young people. Thank goodness for friends who encourage, uplift, and help us be ourselves. Those nine girls will never forget the day they spent making dreams come true!

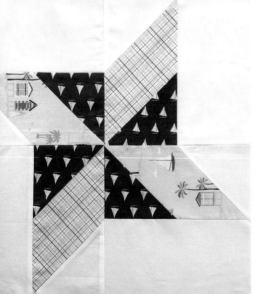

 Here's another colorway of this block. Try different combinations of fabric to see which one you like best.

materials

makes a 64" X 82" quilt

QUILT TOP
- 1 package 10" squares
- 2¾ yards background

BORDER
- 1½ yards

BACKING
- 5 yards

BINDING
- ¾ yard

SAMPLE QUILT
- **Woodland Clearing** by Liesl Gibson
  for Robert Kaufman

1 cut

Select 3 contrasting 10" squares.
Cut:

- 2 print squares in half, making
  (4) 5" x 10" rectangles. Trim
  each to 5" x 9½".

- 1 print square into (4) 5"
  squares.

From the background fabric, cut:

- (4) 5" x 9½" rectangles
- (4) 5" squares

2A

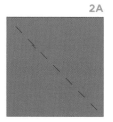

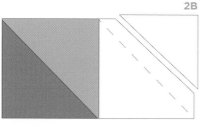

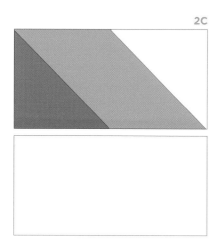

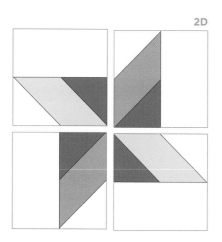

2 sew

Fold a 5″ print square from corner to corner once on the diagonal and lightly press the crease in place to mark your sewing line. Place the square on the left end of a print 5″ x 9½″ rectangle with right sides facing and stitch along the crease. Trim ¼″ away from the seam line. 2A

Fold a 5″ background square from corner to corner once on the diagonal and lightly press the crease in place to mark your sewing line. Place the square on the right end of the print 5″ x 9½″ rectangle with right sides facing and stitch along the crease. Trim ¼″ away from the seam line. **Make 4 units**, always placing the print square on the left end of the rectangle and the background square on the right. 2B

Sew a 5″ x 9½″ background rectangle to each unit. 2C

Sew the units together as shown to complete the block. **Make 12.** 2D

Block Size: 18″ finished

Arrange the blocks into **4 rows** with each row consisting of **3 blocks.** Press the seams of the odd numbered rows toward the left and the even numbered rows toward the right to make the seams nest.

Sew the rows together.

3 border

Cut (8) 5½″ strips across the width of the fabric. Sew the strips together end-to-end to make one long strip. Trim the borders from this strip.

Refer to Borders (pg. 100) in the Construction Basics to measure and cut the outer borders. The strips are approximately 72½″ for the sides and approximately 64½″ for the top and bottom.

4 quilt and bind

Layer the quilt with batting and backing and quilt. After the quilting is complete, square up the quilt and trim away all excess batting and backing. Add binding to complete the quilt. See Construction Basics (pg. 101) for binding instructions.

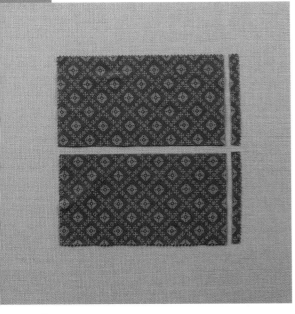

1 Cut (2) 10″ squares in half, then trim to 9½″.

2 Cut a contrasting 10″ square into (4) 5″ squares.

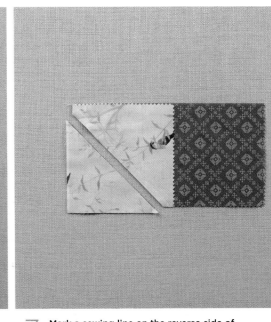

3 Mark a sewing line on the reverse side of a contrasting 5″ square and sew it to one end of a 9½″ rectangle. Trim the excess fabric away ¼″ from the sewn seam.

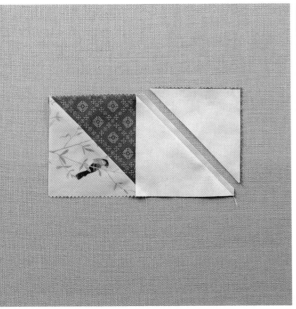

4 Draw a line from corner to corner on the reverse side of a 5″ background square. Sew it to the other end of the rectangle and trim ¼″ away from the sewn line.

5 Sew the rectangle to a background rectangle to complete 1 quadrant of the block.

6 Sew 4 quadrants together to complete the block.

For the tutorial and everything you need to make this quilt visit:
www.msqc.co/blockspring16

crosswalk

quilt designed by JENNY DOAN

When Sarah and Natalie were little girls, we lived in a wonderful old house on the edge of a bluff that overlooked a beautiful expanse of rolling hills in Salinas, California. At times, it felt like we lived out in the country, even in a city of 150,000 people. Home of the famous author, John Steinbeck, this landscape has inspired wonderful stories, beloved by generations. For my girls, it was the perfect setting to develop a keen imagination and an appetite for adventure.

Our neighborhood had a friendly, small town feel. Like all the other homes on our block, we had a low fence that skirted the edge of the yard, and Sarah and Natalie loved to climb up on that fence and sit together to look out over the bluffs and dream up imaginary lives they'd like to live. We read a lot of stories together about children going on adventures all by themselves, and I think these girls had grand fantasies about setting off alone, just like the Boxcar Children. Staring out at those soft, golden hills, they'd imagine a life free from chores and annoying younger siblings—a life filled with galloping horses, charming friends, and colorful parties thrown by wandering bands of gypsies.

The closest the girls ever really got to that kind of freedom, however, was the short walk they took to school. How they ever arrived on time is a mystery, as they spent the entire half-mile journey exploring, imagining, and having wonderful adventures.

crosswalk quilt

A typical week for them might have looked something like this. On Monday, Sarah and Natalie were Olympic gymnasts. The challenge? To complete cartwheel after cartwheel along an entire block with no stopping allowed!

On Tuesday, they were covert spies. Each house they passed was an endless source of mystery and entertainment. Who lived there? What did they do? Did they have dreadful secrets? Were they undercover criminals or even royalty in disguise?

Wednesday, they held tests of bravery. Did they dare to pick up an unknown neighbor's newspaper in the driveway, run it all the way up to the front porch, and race back without getting caught?

They ran as fast as they could on Thursday, all the way to the school building without stopping, arriving at the front doors giddy and pink-cheeked.

And finally, on Friday, they were famous scientists, seeking out the most unusual bugs and flowers they could find along the way.

Each school day, as they reached the edge of our quiet neighborhood, they were met by the friendly crossing guard who greeted them with a hearty "good morning" as he guided them safely across the only busy street on their journey.

I love to think back on those days when our little neighborhood seemed as vast as the whole world, and a journey across the crosswalk held as much adventure as a young mind could imagine.

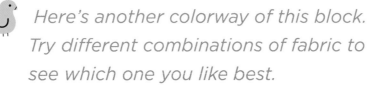

Here's another colorway of this block. Try different combinations of fabric to see which one you like best.

materials

makes a 67" X 80" quilt

QUILT TOP
- 1 roll 2½ print strips
- 2 packages 5" background squares

INSIDE BORDER
- ¾ yard

OUTSIDE BORDER
- 1½ yards

BACKING
- 5 yards

BINDING
- ¾ yard

SAMPLE QUILT
- **True Colors** by Amy Butler for Free Spirit

1 sew

Make a strip set by sewing (5) 2½ strips together. **Make 8.** Press the seam allowances all in the same direction. **1A**

Trim the strips into 4" increments. You should get 10 from each strip set for a **total of 80. 1B**

2 cut

Cut each 5" background square from corner to corner once on the diagonal. You'll need **160 triangles. 2A**

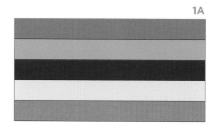

1A

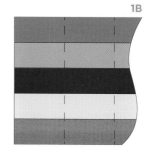

1B

2A

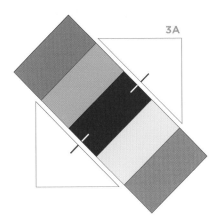

3A

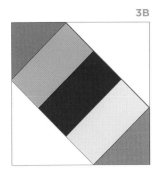

3B

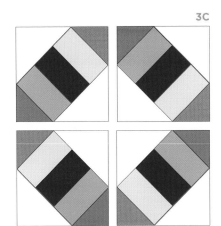

3C

3 sew

Fold a strip set and 2 background triangles in half. Finger press a crease in place to mark each halfway point. Match up the crease in the triangle with the crease in the strip set and sew a background triangle to either side of the strip set. Notice that the triangles don't extend the length of the pieced strip. Because you are trimming the unit, the triangle can be shorter than the strip. (We like saving fabric!) **Make 4 units.** 3A

Trim the block so it measures 7" square. 3B

Sew the 4 units together as shown to make one block. **Make 20.** 3C

Block size: 13" Finished

Lay out the blocks so you have **5 rows** with each row consisting of **4 blocks.** Once you are happy with the arrangement, sew the blocks together into rows. Press all even rows toward the left and all odd rows toward the right to make the seams nest. Sew the rows together.

4 inner border

Cut (7) 2½" strips across the width of the fabric. Sew the strips together end-to-end to make one long strip. Trim the borders from this strip.

Refer to Borders (pg. 100) in the Construction Basics to measure and cut the inner borders. The strips are approximately 65½" for the sides and approximately 56½" for the top and bottom.

5 outer border

Cut (8) 6" strips across the width of the fabric. Sew the strips together end-to-end to make one long strip. Trim the borders from this strip.

Refer to Borders (pg. 100) in the Construction Basics to measure and cut the outer borders. The strips are approximately 69½" for the sides and approximately 67½" for the top and bottom.

6 quilt and bind

Layer the quilt with batting and backing and quilt. After the quilting is complete, square up the quilt and trim away all excess batting and backing. Add binding to complete the quilt. See Construction Basics (pg. 101) for binding instructions.

1 Make a strip set by sewing (5) 2½″ strips together. Trim the strips into 4″ increments.

2 Cut a 5″ square from corner to corner once on the diagonal.

3 Sew a triangle to either side of the strip.

4 Trim the block to 7″ square by aligning your ruler with the background triangles.

5 Press, after trimming.

6 Sew 4 units together to make the block.

For the tutorial and everything you need to make this quilt visit:
www.msqc.co/blockspring16

cheery-o

quilt designed by NATALIE EARNHEART

Raising kids has its joys and its challenges, especially when you're raising seven! Luckily, I've always been a pretty high-energy person, but there have certainly been times when all I wanted in life was a little more sleep. I remember one such morning when the baby was finally sleeping peacefully, though she'd kept me up for most of the night. I was just so desperate for a little shut eye that when the other kids got up, I turned the tv on, handed them a box of cereal to snack on, and collapsed into bed.

A little while later, I emerged from my sleep-coma to find that my floor was no longer visible under a thick carpet of Cheerios! I was exhausted. I hadn't showered in days, and now my house was being taken over by cereal! I felt like crying, screaming, or pulling my hair out by the roots. Maybe all three? But before I could even choose which kind of meltdown to have, my chubby-cheeked three-year-old threw a handful of Cheerios in the air and yelled, "Surprise!"

The way she said it made me pause. She was so earnest in her celebration; she really thought I would see this disaster as a reason to party, and it was adorable. She was still in her fuzzy pajamas, she had Cheerios in her hair, and I

realized that as annoying as it was going to be to clean up the contents of an entire box of cereal, in the future, when I looked back on this moment, I wouldn't be mad. I would just miss the days when my babies were so little. So, I didn't yell. I didn't cry. I hugged my daughter instead.

I try to remember that moment of clarity amid the Cheerios whenever I find myself feeling discouraged. So often frustrations come from things that turn out to be blessings. When I'm in a hurry, annoyed with a project, or overwhelmed by a mess, it just means that my life is full of good things and I need to look at it with more grateful eyes. That's the best way I've learned to find joy in everyday life.

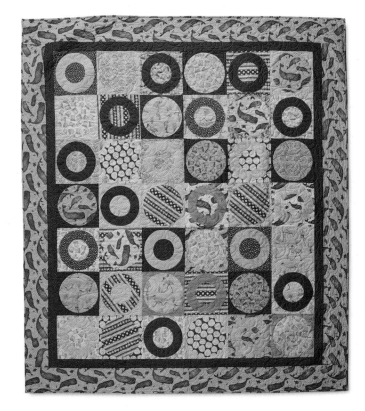

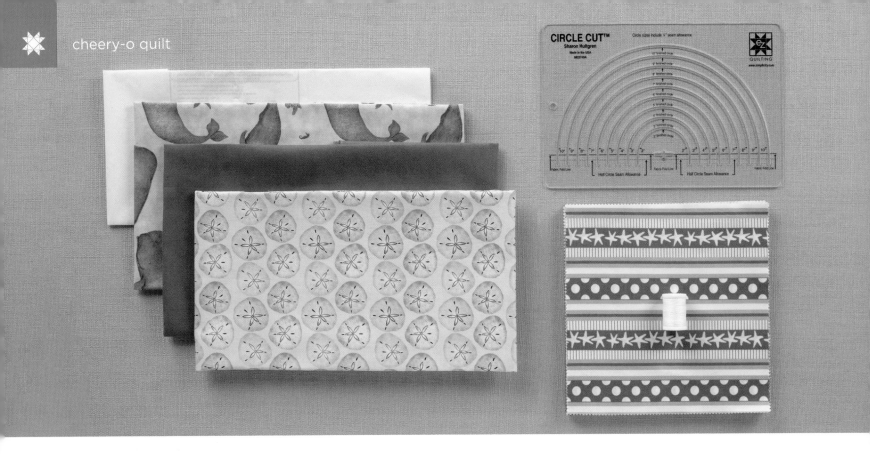

materials
makes a 63" X 72½" quilt

QUILT TOP
- 2 packages 10" squares
- 4¾ yards paper-backed fusible web

OPTIONAL TOOLS
- Easy Circle Cut ruler
- Easy Circle Cut rotary cutter

BORDER
- 1 yard

BACKING
- 4 yards

BINDING
- ¾ yard

SAMPLE QUILT
- **Barnacle Bay** by Debbi Hubbs for Studio E

before you begin
Apply fusible web to fabric before cutting the circles and donuts (template on page 87). If you are using the Easy Circle Cut ruler to make the donut, cut an 8" circle, then cut a 4" circle out of the center of the 8" circle. Set the 4" circles aside to use in our bonus project.

1 cut
From assorted print squares, cut:
- 21 circles
- 21 donuts

1A

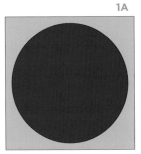

1B

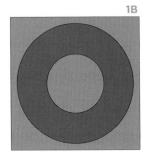

2 block assembly

Peel the paper backing from the reverse side of a circle and center it on a contrasting 10" square. Fuse and machine appliqué in place using a blanket stitch or any other decorative stitch of your choice. **Make 21 circle blocks** as shown. 1A

Peel the paper backing from the reverse side of a donut and center it on a contrasting 10" square. Fuse and machine appliqué in place using a blanket stitch or any other decorative stitch of your choice. **Make 21 donut blocks** as shown. 1B

3 quilt assembly

Lay out the blocks in 7 rows with each row containing 6 blocks. Begin the odd numbered rows with a donut block and alternate with a circle block. Begin the even numbered rows with a circle block and alternate with a donut block. Sew the blocks together then join the rows.

4 border

Cut (7) 3½" strips across the width of the fabric. Sew the strips together end-to-end to make one long strip. Trim the borders from this strip.

Refer to Borders (pg. 100) in the Construction Basics to measure and cut the borders. The strips are approximately 67" for the sides and approximately 63½" for the top and bottom.

5 quilt and bind

Layer the quilt with batting and backing and quilt. After the quilting is complete, square up the quilt and trim away all excess batting and backing. Add binding to complete the quilt. See Construction Basics (pg. 101) for binding instructions.

5A

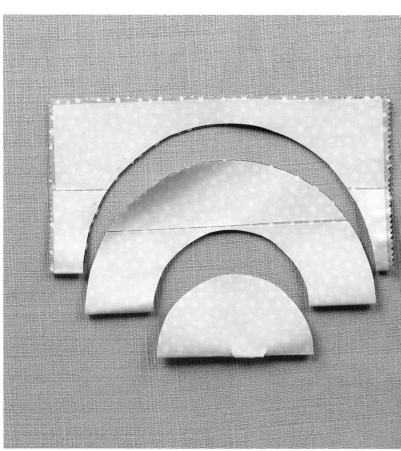

1 Apply fusible web to each 10″ square you are using for circles and donuts.

2 Cut one large circle and one small circle from the center to make the donut block.

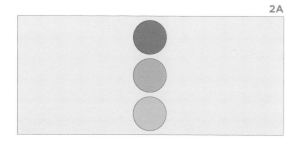

2A

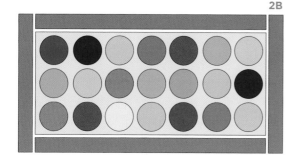

2B

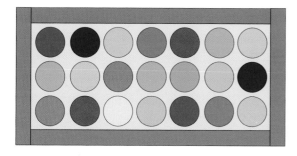

BONUS PROJECT: TABLE RUNNER

materials

makes a 20" X 40" table runner

TABLE RUNNER TOP
(21) 4" circles – we used the leftover circles from our Cheery-O Quilt

BACKGROUND
½ yard fabric

BORDER
½ yard – includes binding

BACKING
¾ yard

1 cut

From the background fabric, cut:

- (1) 16½" x 36½" rectangle

Fold the rectangle in half vertically and horizontally. Lightly press in a crease to mark the center of the rectangle.

2 assembly

Peel the paper backing from the reverse side of the small circles. Place 3 circles vertically on the center crease of the background fabric spaced an equal distance apart. Remember to allow ¼" on each side for the seam allowance. Press in place when you have them spaced as you wish. **2A**

Add 3 rows of circles to either side of the center row. Press in place when you are happy with the arrangement taking into account the ¼" seam allowance. Appliqué in place using a buttonhole stitch or any other decorative stitch of your choice. **2B**

3 border

Measure the length of the table runner, and cut (2) 2½" strips to that measurement. (Even though we know we cut the piece 36½", it's a good idea to measure again because the appliqué can sometimes take up some the of length and width.)

Sew a border strip to either long side of the center of the table runner.

Measure the table runner through the center vertically. Be sure to include the two border strips. Cut (2) 2½" rectangles to your measurement. Sew one to either end of the table runner.

4 quilt and bind

Layer the table runner with batting and backing and quilt. After the quilting is complete, square it up and trim away all excess batting and backing. Add binding to complete the runner. See Construction Basics (pg. 101) for binding instructions.

Circle template is actual size - Copy this image and cut out to use as a template. Trace on interfacing.

87

FROM A FAT QUARTER (18" x 22")

you can cut the following PRECUTS:

2½" strip			
5" square	5" square	5" square	5" square
5" square	5" square	5" square	5" square
5" square	5" square	5" square	5" square

(12) 5" squares + (1) 2½" strip

2½" strip	
2½" strip	
2½" strip	
10" square	10" square

(2) 10" squares + (3) 2½" strips

2½" strip
2½" strip
2½" strip
2½" strip
2½" strip
2½" strip
2½" strip

(7) 2½" strips

2½" strip			
5" square	5" square	5" square	5" square
10" square		10" square	

(2) 10" squares + (4) 5" squares + (1) 2½" strip

how to cut a fat quarter

Quilters love fabric of all shapes and sizes, but one of our favorites is the fat quarter. Some have even called it "the original precut." It's just a great little piece of fabric that can be used in many different ways. You'll often find beautiful stacks of fat quarters bundled together with pretty ribbons, all ready for your next project. Although they look great on the shelf, you might be thinking to yourself, "How do I actually use them?" Well, you're in luck, because we have some answers for you.

If you're wondering what a fat quarter is, it's a wide quarter yard of fabric. When a yard of fabric is cut in half across the width and then that half yard is cut down the middle, this time lengthwise, it produces a wider quarter yard, instead of a thinner quarter yard—a typical quarter yard of fabric measures 9" x 44" inches, whereas a fat quarter measures 18" x 22". It's the same amount of fabric, but the

other 18" x 22" CUTS:

2½"	2½"	2½"	2½"	2½"	2½"	2½"	2½"
2½"	2½"	2½"	2½"	2½"	2½"	2½"	2½"
2½"	2½"	2½"	2½"	2½"	2½"	2½"	2½"
2½"	2½"	2½"	2½"	2½"	2½"	2½"	2½"
2½"	2½"	2½"	2½"	2½"	2½"	2½"	2½"
2½"	2½"	2½"	2½"	2½"	2½"	2½"	2½"
2½"	2½"	2½"	2½"	2½"	2½"	2½"	2½"

(56) 2½" squares

3"	3"	3"	3"	3"	3"	3"
3"	3"	3"	3"	3"	3"	3"
3"	3"	3"	3"	3"	3"	3"
3"	3"	3"	3"	3"	3"	3"
3"	3"	3"	3"	3"	3"	3"
3"	3"	3"	3"	3"	3"	3"

(36) 3" squares

4½" square	4½" square	4½" square	4½" square
4½" square	4½" square	4½" square	4½" square
4½" square	4½" square	4½" square	4½" square
4½" square	4½" square	4½" square	4½" square

(16) 4½" squares

6" square	6" square	6" square
6" square	6" square	6" square
6" square	6" square	6" square

(9) 6" squares

very little waste. In addition, with large-scale prints, you're more likely to get the entire design in your cut. Fat quarters also allow you to cut longer strips along the length of the fabric, parallel to the selvage edge, which causes less stretching. Fat quarters offer much more flexibility to work with the direction of the print—like with vertical stripes. They are also perfect for sampler quilts, when you need a lot of different colors or prints, and they're an easy way to begin building your fabric stash.

Let's chat about how many pieces you can cut from just one fat quarter. There's quite a few possibilities! We love precut fabrics, and so many of our quilts use them, so we've drawn up some charts to help you see how many 2½", 5", and 10" pieces you can get from one fat quarter. Then you can take that beautiful stash and use it much more effectively. So grab those fat quarters and let's get quilting!

pieces are different shapes. This size is more versatile for quilters; it can be cut into many different shapes. You can use fat quarters for projects that require pieces larger than 9" wide. For example, if you needed a 16" square of fabric, you would have to cut up a half yard of fabric and then you'd have quite a bit left over, but if you used a fat quarter instead, you would have just the right amount with

4-patch & strips

QUILT SIZE
75" X 88"

DESIGNED BY
Jenny Doan

PIECED BY
Carol Henderson

QUILTED BY
Debbie Allen

QUILT TOP
1 roll print 2½" strips
1 roll background 2½" strips *or*
   3 yards background fabric

BORDER
1¼ yards

BACKING
5½ yards

BINDING
¾ yard

SAMPLE QUILT
Enchanted by Alisse Courter
   for Camelot

ONLINE TUTORIALS
msqc.co/blockspring16

QUILTING
Bo Dangle

PATTERN
pg. 32

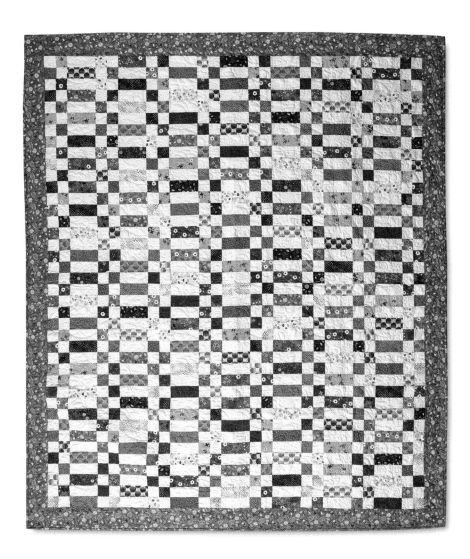

cheery-o

QUILT SIZE
63" X 72½"

DESIGNED BY
Natalie Earnheart

PIECED BY
Jenny Doan

QUILTED BY
Kara Snow

QUILT TOP
2 packages 10" squares
4¾ yards paper-backed fusible web

OPTIONAL TOOLS
Easy Circle Cut ruler
Easy Circle Cut rotary cutter

BORDER
1 yard

BACKING
4 yards

BINDING
¾ yard

SAMPLE QUILT
Barnacle Bay by Debbi Hubbs
 for Studio E

ONLINE TUTORIALS
msqc.co/blockspring16

QUILTING
Free Swirls

PATTERN
pg. 80

crosswalk

QUILT SIZE
67" X 80"

DESIGNED BY
Jenny Doan

PIECED BY
Carol Henderson

QUILTED BY
Abigail Anderson

QUILT TOP
1 roll 2½ print strips
2 packages 5" background squares

INSIDE BORDER
¾ yard

OUTSIDE BORDER
1½ yards

BACKING
5 yards

BINDING
¾ yard

SAMPLE QUILT
True Colors by Amy Butler
   for Free Spirit

ONLINE TUTORIALS
msqc.co/blockspring16

QUILTING
Posies

PATTERN
pg. 72

disappearing
4-patch star

QUILT SIZE
82" X 94"

DESIGNED BY
Jenny Doan

PIECED BY
Carol Henderson

QUILTED BY
Debbie Allen

QUILT TOP
2 packages 5" print squares
1½ yards coordinating fabric
3½ yards background fabric-
   includes inner border

OUTER BORDER
1½ yards

BACKING
7½ yards

BINDING
¾ yard

SAMPLE QUILT
Wordsmith by Janet Clare for Moda

ONLINE TUTORIALS
msqc.co/blockspring16

QUILTING
Cotton Seed

PATTERN
pg. 8

friendship
pinwheel

QUILT SIZE
64" X 82"

DESIGNED BY
Jenny Doan

PIECED BY
Kelly McKenzie

QUILTED BY
Karen Russell, Kayla Youtsey

QUILT TOP
1 package 10" squares
2¾ yards background

BORDER
1½ yards

BACKING
5 yards

BINDING
¾ yard

SAMPLE QUILT
Woodland Clearing by Liesl Gibson
for Robert Kaufman

ONLINE TUTORIALS
msqc.co/blockspring16

QUILTING
Daisy Days

PATTERN
pg. 64

ingrid's garden

QUILT SIZE
92" X 106¼"

DESIGNED BY
Natalie Earnheart

PIECED BY
Cindy Morris

QUILTED BY
Raven Rhoads, Dixie Flamm

QUILT TOP
2 packages 10" print squares
4 yards solid – includes inner border

OUTER BORDER
2 yards

BACKING
8¼ yards

BINDING
¾ yard

ADDITIONAL SUPPLIES
1 MSQC 10" Half-Hexagon Template

SAMPLE QUILT
Whisper by Victoria Johnson for Windham

ONLINE TUTORIALS
msqc.co/blockwinter16

QUILTING
Curly Twirly Flowers

QUILT PATTERN
pg. 24

ohio star

QUILT SIZE
88" X 100½"

DESIGNED BY
Jenny Doan

PIECED BY
Cindy Morris

QUILTED BY
Mari Zullig, Kara Snow

QUILT TOP
3 packages (42 count) 5" print
squares
6 yards background fabric –
includes sashing strips

BORDER
• 2 yards - includes cornerstones

BACKING
• 8 yards

BINDING
• ¾ yard

SAMPLE QUILT
• **Beaujolais** by Sue Daley Designs

ONLINE TUTORIALS
msqc.co/blockspring16

QUILTING
Paisley Feather

QUILT PATTERN
pg. 56

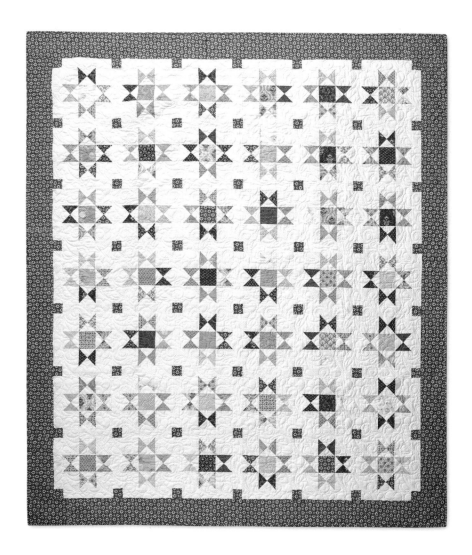

quatrefoil star

QUILT SIZE
74" X 86"

DESIGNED BY
Jenny Doan

PIECED BY
Cindy Morris

QUILTED BY
Tia Gilliam

QUILT TOP
4 packages of 5" print squares
2¾ yards white – includes inner
    border
1¼ yards coordinating print

OUTER BORDER
1¼ yards

BACKING
5¼ yards

BINDING
¾ yard

SAMPLE QUILT
Bees 'n Blooms by Kansas Troubles
    for Moda

ONLINE TUTORIALS
msqc.co/blockspring16

QUILTING
Paisley Feather

PATTERN
pg. 48

sashed half-hexagon

QUILT SIZE
50" X 63"

DESIGNED BY
Natalie Earnheart

PIECED BY
Cindy Morris

QUILTED BY
Dixie Flamm

QUILT TOP
1 package 10" squares
1½ yards sashing fabric – *we used gray*

BORDER
1 yard

BACKING
3¼ yards

BINDING
½ yard

ADDITIONAL SUPPLIES
1 MSQC 10" Half-Hexagon Template

SAMPLE QUILT
Sunday Ride by Cheri Guidry for Benartex/Contempo

ONLINE TUTORIALS
msqc.co/blockspring16

QUILTING
Flowers

PATTERN
pg. 16

tangled geese

QUILT SIZE
70" X 78"

DESIGNED BY
Jenny Doan

PIECED BY
Carol Henderson

QUILTED BY
Mari Zullig

QUILT TOP
1 roll print 2½" strips
4¼ yards background fabric –
  includes inner border

OUTER BORDER
1½ yards

BACKING
4¾ yards

BINDING
¾ yard

SAMPLE QUILT
Circle Play by Ann Lauer for
  Benartex

ONLINE TUTORIALS
msqc.co/blockspring16

QUILTING
Loops & Swirls

PATTERN
pg. 40

construction basics

- All seams are ¼" inch unless directions specify differently.

- Cutting instructions are given at the point when cutting is required.

- Precuts are not prewashed; therefore do not prewash other fabrics in the project

- All strips are cut WOF

- Remove all selvages

- All yardages based on 42" WOF

ACRONYMS USED

MSQC	Missouri Star Quilt Co.
RST	right sides together
WST	wrong sides together
HST	half-square triangle
WOF	width of fabric
LOF	length of fabric

pre-cut glossary

5" SQUARE PACK
1 = (42) 5" squares or ¾ yd of fabric
1 = baby
2 = crib
3 = lap
4 = twin

2½" STRIP ROLL
1 = (40) 2½" strip roll cut the width of fabric
    or 2¾ yds of fabric
1 = a twin
2 = queen

10" SQUARE PACK
1 = (42) 10" square pack of fabric: 2¾ yds total
1 = a twin
2 = queen

When we mention a precut, we are basing the pattern on a 40-42 count pack. Not all precuts have the same count, so be sure to check the count on your precut to make sure you have enough pieces to complete your project.

general quilting

- All seams are ¼" inch unless directions specify differently.
- Cutting instructions are given at the point when cutting is required.
- Precuts are not prewashed; therefore do not prewash other fabrics in the project.
- All strips are cut width of fabric.
- Remove all selvages.
- All yardages based on 42" width of fabric (WOF).

press seams

- Use the cotton setting on your iron when pressing.
- Press the seam just as it was sewn RST. This "sets" the seam.
- To set the seam, press just as it was sewn with right sides together.
- With dark fabric on top, lift the dark fabric and press back.
- The seam allowance is pressed toward the dark side. Some patterns may direct otherwise for certain situations.
- Press toward borders. Pieced borders may demand otherwise.
- Press diagonal seams open on binding to reduce bulk.

borders

- Always measure the quilt top 3 times before cutting borders.
- Start measuring about 4" in from each side and through the center vertically.
- Take the average of those 3 measurements.
- Cut 2 border strips to that size. Piece strips together if needed.
- Attach one to either side of the quilt.
- Position the border fabric on top as you sew. The feed dogs can act like rufflers. Having the border on top will prevent waviness and keep the quilt straight.
- Repeat this process for the top and bottom borders, measuring the width 3 times.
- Include the newly attached side borders in your measurements.
- Press toward the borders.

binding

find a video tutorial at: www.msqc.co/006

- Use 2½" strips for binding.
- Sew strips end-to-end into one long strip with diagonal seams, aka plus sign method (next). Press seams open.
- Fold in half lengthwise wrong sides together and press.
- The entire length should equal the outside dimension of the quilt plus 15" - 20."

plus sign method

- Lay one strip across the other as if to make a plus sign right sides together.
- Sew from top inside to bottom outside corners crossing the intersections of fabric as you sew. Trim excess to ¼" seam allowance.
- Press seam open.

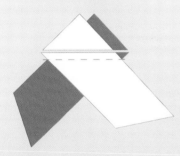

attach binding

- Match raw edges of folded binding to the quilt top edge.
- Leave a 10" tail at the beginning.
- Use a ¼" seam allowance.
- Start in the middle of a long straight side.

find a video tutorial at: www.msqc.co/001

10" tail   ¼"

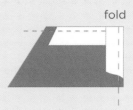

90°   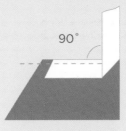   fold

miter corners

- Stop sewing ¼" before the corner.
- Move the quilt out from under the presser foot.
- Clip the threads.
- Flip the binding up at a 90° angle to the edge just sewn.
- Fold the binding down along the next side to be sewn, aligning raw edges.
- The fold will lie along the edge just completed.
- Begin sewing on the fold.

close binding

*MSQC recommends **The Binding Tool** from TQM Products to finish binding perfectly every time.*

- Stop sewing when you have 12" left to reach the start.
- Where the binding tails come together, trim excess leaving only 2½" of overlap.
- It helps to pin or clip the quilt together at the two points where the binding starts and stops. This takes the pressure off of the binding tails while you work.
- Use the plus sign method to sew the two binding ends together, except this time when making the plus sign, match the edges. Using a pencil, mark your sewing line because you won't be able to see where the corners intersect. Sew across.

plus sign with matched edges

- Trim off excess; press seam open.
- Fold in half wrong sides together, and align all raw edges to the quilt top.
- Sew this last binding section to the quilt. Press.
- Turn the folded edge of the binding around to the back of the quilt and tack into place with an invisible stitch or machine stitch if you wish.

THE FAIR THIEF

PART 1

Quilting Scandal

—— *A JENNY DOAN MYSTERY* ——

written by Steve Westover

The aromatic bouquet of cut grass, livestock, and funnel cakes distracted Jenny for just a moment before she forced herself to refocus. She held the clipboard against her chest as she leaned in closer. Jenny cocked her head and squinted her eyes as she examined the stitching on the vibrant quilt depicting a seaside village and ocean waves. Biting her pen, the cap flattened between her teeth and then she took a step back. She raised her hand and waited for the two other judges to join her.

"Magnificent!" the first judge gushed as she examined the quilt. The other judge nodded in agreement.

Jenny also agreed but then raised a finger. "There's no doubt it's beautiful but ... "

Stephanie McIntyre, a rising twenty-something quilting phenom, exhaled with an exasperated huff. "But what? What is it now?"

As usual, a smile came easily to Jenny's face as she considered how to break the bad news. "Well, I'm sorry to say that this quilt doesn't qualify for this particular competition. It's gorgeous and well-crafted and I'm sure it could do well in the 'right' competition."

Stephanie shook her head slowly. "And why doesn't it qualify? Please tell."

Jenny pointed toward the corner of the quilt with the chewed end of her pen. "Sure, it's an original design but it clearly isn't hand-stitched. This was done on a longarm stitcher with a pattern used to imitate an imperfect, handquilted appearance.

Stephanie's eyes widened as she considered the bombshell news. Both judges leaned closer as Jenny explained.

"You'll notice the stitches aren't perfectly straight and the spacing is slightly uneven so that it appears to have been done by hand. But if you compare the stitching on the vertical edge of this corner to the horizontal edge, you'll see that the unevenness is identical. It's actually an ingenious pattern," Jenny explained. "See, look right here." Noticing the unsightliness of the chewed pen Jenny stuck it to her clipboard and traced the stitches with her finger.

"Well, I'll be," proclaimed Martha, the eldest of the quilting judges. "You're right, Jenny. Stephanie, what do you think?" All three judges agreed. Martha paused for a moment before pulling a red tag from her bag. She wrote 'disqualified' on the tag and pinned it to the quilt. "It's such a pity."

"Yes it is." Jenny cleared her throat gently, "But I'm happy a deserving quilter, one who followed the rules, will get the recognition she deserves. If you'll excuse me I need just a few more minutes to do a final review and then tabulate my scores. Are you ladies almost finished?" Jenny asked. Both judges affirmed they were nearly done. "Great. Let's finish up and present the awards by 5:00. That gives us half an hour. Sound good?"

Both women agreed. Jenny coughed into her sleeve and then wiped a line of perspiration from her hairline.

"Are you feeling alright, sweetie?" Martha asked.

Jenny forced a smile. "Let's just say that I won't mind finishing up and getting back to my hotel room."

Jenny made one last pass around the circus tent-turned quilt gallery, first along the quilt-lined edges and then among the numerous rows. After completing her scoring, Jenny gathered with Stephanie and Martha to determine the winners.

Sitting in a chair near the microphone, Jenny rested while the others pinned the ribbons to the winning quilts. She leaned forward, hunching over as her stomach churned. Her breathing became slow and deep as she tried to ignore the odors of the state fair pressing against her. She closed her eyes for a moment and then opened them slowly.

"Jenny? Are you ready?" Stephanie asked.

"She's not feeling well," Martha said. "Give her a moment."

Stephanie frowned slightly to express sympathy but then her eyes brightened. "You know Jenny, if you're not feeling up to announcing the awards I'd be happy to do it for you."

Jenny detected Stephanie's selfish intention but considered the offer anyways. After a brief hesitation she stood slowly and grinned. "Thank you, but I can manage."

The only thing Jenny loved more than quilting, and perhaps singing, was talking to people. Personal interactions energized her in a way she couldn't fully describe, but it was something she always looked forward to and in turn, others looked forward to meeting her. She stood at the microphone, eager to congratulate the winners who had entered their work in in the State's annual Quilt Fair. She read the names of each winner and joined in with the applause of the crowd as she handed each their certificate and check. Instead of offering her usual hug, she quickly explained she wasn't feeling well and offered to bump elbows instead but each of the winners hugged her anyway. The quilters beamed with

pride when Jenny announced that their labors of love would be displayed in the State Rotunda for an entire month following the fair. Jenny couldn't have been more pleased.

Five minutes after the awards ceremony ended Jenny's assistant, MK, rushed her back to the hotel for rest and recuperation. Jenny sipped on ginger ale but wasn't ready to eat. She turned on a Kansas City Royals baseball game and fell asleep.

By morning the bug had passed and Jenny felt like a new woman. MK marveled at the quantity and variety of Jenny's breakfast: eggs over easy with toast, grits, bacon, and waffles.

"I see you're feeling well," MK said while smirking playfully. "Do you want anything else? A cookie? A gallon of chocolate milk, perhaps?"

Jenny raised one scolding eyebrow followed by her usual smile. "So what's on our schedule today?"

"I thought we'd enjoy some time exploring the fair before heading home," MK said. "Aside from the quilting, we didn't get much of a chance to look around yesterday and I'm dying for a funnel cake. Our flight doesn't leave 'til 8:30 tonight."

Jenny's stomach lurched at the mention of 'funnel cake' and the memory of all the state fair's competing aromas. After a moment of concentration and two deep breaths she felt fine again. "Or we could head over to the outlet mall and do some shopping."

MK's lips puckered as she prepared a counter offer. "Or maybe we could … "

THUMP. THUMP. THUMP. The harsh knock on the restaurant window startled Jenny and caused MK to leap from her seat. "Jenny!" Stephanie called through the glass.

Jenny waved for her fellow quilting judge to come in and join them, which Stephanie quickly did. "You won't believe what happened," Stephanie said anxiously. Before MK or Jenny could proffer a guess, Stephanie continued. She lowered her voice to a whisper. "I'm so glad I found you. Something strange is afoot."

MK folded her arms and stared at the gossipy woman. "Rather dramatic. What nefarious activity is 'afoot', exactly?" MK asked flatly.

Stephanie paused for a moment as she leaned closer. "The top four quilts from yesterday—they're all gone."

Jenny stopped nibbling at the corner of her toast as her jaw dropped. Her brow furrowed. "No! That's awful. What a shame."

"Stolen? How valuable would those quilts be?" MK asked.

"Oh, they're valuable," Stephanie replied, "but likely more sentimental than financial."

Jenny shook her head. "The hours spent designing and piecing ... Who would do such a thing?"

"I spoke to each of the winning quilters this morning," Stephanie said. "They're upset and disappointed."

"Of course. I would be too," Jenny said. "What can be done?"

Stephanie bit at the corner of her lip and chuckled softly. "I'm glad you asked."

"Oh?" MK looked skeptical.

Stephanie glanced at MK and then back at Jenny. "You have a bit of a reputation for ... solving certain kinds of problems." Jenny exhaled a deep breath as her eyes met MK's.

"Apparently I have a reputation."

MK shrugged. "Yep. You do."

"It's a good one, I hope," Jenny said, knowing where the conversation was leading.

Stephanie nodded. "Of course. You're the Jessica Fletcher of the quilting world. Your work solving the murder at the quilting conference in Portland a couple of years ago is legendary and then you saved that woman while bringing down a dirty businessman and his thugs.

"It's, well, it's ... " Stephanie waved her hands wildly as she searched for the right words.

Jenny remained calm as she tried to fight off the embarrassment of realizing her crime fighting exploits were known within the quilting world. "My role in those things has been greatly exaggerated, I assure you."

Stephanie looked to MK who was shaking her head. MK muttered. "Sorry, Jenny. Not exaggerated at all."

Stephanie took courage. "I'd never want to put you in danger but this is on a totally different level than murders. It's safe. Cross my heart. I really need your help. The police have been contacted but stolen quilts aren't a high priority for them. But to the quilters it's a huge deal. It's their time and original designs, lost forever, maybe. Jenny, will you help me find the quilts and return them to their owners? I want them to be rewarded for their hard work, not sucker punched by some petty thief. I want their beautiful quilts displayed at the Capitol. I want these quilters to get the attention and praise they've earned."

While Jenny stared at her toast, contemplating the request, MK spoke up. "Of course Jenny will help you." MK then looked nervously at Jenny. "Right?"

Jenny appreciated MK's desire to help and Stephanie's passion for justice. Jenny smiled. "You are absolutely right. We're going to find those quilts and return them to the winners before our flight leaves tonight. So, let's get cracking!"